Exercises in Lip Pointing

OTHER BOOKS BY ANNHARTE

Being On the Moon (1990)

Columbus Coyote Café (1994)

EXERCISES IN LIP POINTING

ANNHARTE

NEW STAR BOOKS
VANCOUVER
2003

New Star Books Ltd.
107 - 3477 Commercial Street
Vancouver, BC V5N 4E8
www.NewStarBooks.com
info@NewStarBooks.com

Cover by Rayola Graphic Design
Cover painting by Rebecca Belmore
Typesetting by New Star Books
Printed & bound in Canada by Gauvin Press
First published January 2003. Reprinted September 2003

Publication of this work is made possible by grants from the Canada Council, the British Columbia Arts Council, and the Department of Canadian Heritage Book Publishing Industry Development Program.

Le Conseil des Arts | The Canada Council
du Canada | for the Arts

BRITISH
COLUMBIA
ARTS COUNCIL

NATIONAL LIBRARY OF CANADA CATALOGUING IN PUBLICATION DATA

Baker, Marie Annharte, 1942-
  Exercises in lip pointing / Marie Annharte Baker.

  Poems.
  ISBN 0-921586-92-2

  I. Title.
PS8553.A384E93 2003   C811'.54   C2002-911380-6
PR9199.3.B3438E93 2003

Contents

MEMORY FISHES

Auntie I Dream

*For my aunties, Jemima and Christina
and mother, Sophia, and Granny Emma Jane*

lineup at the potluck
plate full of macaroni
choice of all kinds of meat
rabbit is old favorite
here I was 500 miles due south
distanced dilemma
feeling out of place
among none of my relatives

no last visit to an auntie
she passed away at home with family
they told me she did ask about me
why I saw her spirit stand
on a road turn & wave goodbye
she had a kerchief on her head
saw all this with eyes closed tight
after I bit down on frybread with jam

after Auntie Christina died
we sat on her lumpy bed
spread photographs from boxes
picked one for keepsakes

one time she asked me to help her
put a jigsaw puzzle together

outside the cabin in the bush
a snapshot taken of Christina caught
putting her arm around my dad
both perched on a 24 case of beer
she teased my mom about her new man
a big sister joke I don't forget

my rainbow dream has three sisters
they clean white fish on the sand shore
we kids watch them scrape off scales
fish writhe flip over and lift tails
scales stick to skin
tiny lake mirrors
catch sparkles throw shimmer into eyes

a rainbow arcs over busy aunties
grandchildren tumble on blanket
legs over legs kick up shells
sticky fingers reach for hands
touch face, lips, hair, ears and nose
I listen for each excited heart beat

Half Light Weir I Lie Down

half light   I lie down
silver streaks   flash   shimmer
scaly sides waver
glint in this weir
disappear

glow eye
push back knots
     enter net
     fin in out
     re-enter

     slippage
slide up over each other
     memory fishes
whatever my species
  settles to the bottom
I forget why
throughout history

what is known   where I lie
    is recorded in clay

dream canal

     help me take back land
        attack
red out
red riot
     red right

red writing
red people read
rights read out

red clay tablets   inscribe
taste of smooth fossil
salt of human   inhuman sweat
secret memorials
        I must ingest
                vitamin mineral
supplements   for I endure
        another wake dream
long mourning rushes
        morning again
red clay cannibal
red clay eater
soul sediments flavor
full stomach digest
                weir I lie down
        half light has life

Blueberry Canoe

flirty wind tugged at her blanket
whispered "let's play"

she told him "go away I fast for my vision"
tucked the blanket ends around her knees
he pried out a diamond from a lone star on her back
twirled and put it on a pine branch
murmured "just like a puzzle"
he took every shape she thought hers
saved the bear paws for last
gathered hatchets, arrows and trails
didn't know what was missing
he blew a chill under her rib cage
made shoulders hunch but she knew he still hunted

her grand design had been Moon Over Tipi
she escaped a mother's discipline
over those blueberries in a canoe
it was the biggest souvenir hanging on the tripod
tourists laughed at purple creation she made
her mother lost a dollar sale

a hole in her memory when her mother left
a suitcase of shells beads and a moosehide vest
strange toys for a kid's play
instead she played secretary
pushed old papers under the sewing machine
presser foot up treadled her invoices
bills of lading cancelled cheques

"stop it Windy" she said abruptly
he got too damn close to the tipi
in the back of her mind
with the moon
over his head too
she amused herself
with Twotimer
too much timely

nevermind
didn't spoil her history
might undo few stitches
wouldn't unravel her mind

Cherries Could Be a Girl's Best

diamonds evolve from compost
lush foliage submits in decay
rotting vegetation turns bituminous
coal changes to diamond hard carbon
pressure makes hardest brittle surface radiant
press of flesh
time to force this girl
give up soft belly flab
help find one spot in miles of bush
conceal camouflage panties torn apart

cover up I confess unnecessary nosiness
invade someone else's diary as needed
how white boy lips made best friend more popular
tallied up all conquests except total of me equals none
our diaries hid the usual secrets made known
like if someday a storage vault is cracked open
all good time girls flowers pressed flat
between yellowed newspaper clippings
should crumble because no ladies keep
forged sad confessionals, do they?
turquoise colored inkblots
afterthoughts kiss kiss kisses
squeezed in scrawled overwrites
boastful daring exploit after favorite gripe
top off should be born white lies

right place kept place no time for composite poems
exception a precious envisioning of diamond
why because I liked chemistry in school
equations were balanced to the smallest particle

all diaries of what was aw forget it youth
got tossed into furnace why not go to hell
burnt offerings to unknown goddess of spite
one damn date complete without orgasm
didn't happen to work out in best interests
left was remains of crudest imagination
helluvalotta flames to burn up wickedness
sunday school teaching and bible reading warned
shame stalks a woman from her last cherry night
I coax back cherry babe flames
please come back tonight show sparks
none of the withdrawal — keep me hot stoked
stay for as long words take to fossilize on page
release at the count of three
scary hips held down
I don't want to hold out hold back hold in
cherry scream defiant silence
stop movement inside I might tear
jump out of my skin

don't don't do that
don't don't do that

Dragonfly Real Estate

side of road see how a tub was thrown out
after the job done to collect summer rain
car seat lost stuffing to become ass wipe
nothing to read catalogue pages went quick
leaves rub off characteristic green color
rotting deerhide on the stump is found art
antlers point right over to the Labatts box
grey pulp squashed indicator of party
house if not then evidence old cars
arranged in chronological order of used
to the right over by my lip not four directions
rain fall wash and dry or snow damp seasons
barn wood look on plank walkway with mud clumps
a couple of dragonflies flit overhead
the lady one drops down to fix flex
silver flecked net wings red velvet body

In the Picture I Don't See

in the home of a pink lady
with a pink & grey decor
I sit on a mexican blanket
draped over a grey loveseat
a thin rosy pink stripe
offsets blue & black geometric
runs parallel then intersects a line
that points to my crotch
pink ruffled curtains
match with a pink carpet complement
grey endtables are coordinated by
grey & pink flowered mirrors hang
on the wall above my head

I am a slight off pink accent
a shade of blush soon overtakes
welfare blues hidden by too sharp
contrast for an undertone of shame
feel temporarily out of place
in an ostentatious perhaps typical
mohawk warrior residence
maybe I have wigwam wonder
"who lives here &
am I at all related to them?"

I explore a chinese ceramic vase
on the window ledge & discover
what must be a huge porcelain egg
ready to birth another color scheme
a more pretentious decor
concoct a life style change
the kind I might replicate

if given greater opportunity to deposit
grey deadskin remains
on the sides of the pink bathtub

outside the pink lady's house
the weeds grow taller when watched
shade under the umbrella table
invites the wanderer to park
in an unoccupied zone on the sundeck
the backyard is wild and gives the visitor
strange comfort plus excellent camouflage
easy to see how "SQ combat" might occur
a safari among foxtails might recover
herds of buffalo and lost conquistadores

her backyard is big as a continent
the pink lady returned from Pocono
a neo-rococo lovers' hideaway
her souvenir photo makes me gush
how complete with pink husband
posed in a champagne glass bubble
smiling they hug tight together
in a heartshaped whirlpool tub
both in bed show an awkward shoot
the honeymoon camera is voyeur
strictly bogus but it does reveal
the potential of a threesome view

pink husband assures me
painted Indian babies are real
ceramic plate reproductions
my "papoose girl" fantasies compete
get trapped in a clock campsite
will the tiny tipi leave a ring
I assume her teary eye results not
from piling up the travois to move on
her cause different from my unrest

brought on by 3 a.m. drunk drivers
who argue point at bumpers
threaten my sainthood like Kateri
I am part
Mohawk church lady woman who patrols
but whatever disturbs me is forgotten
the next day when more crisis ensues

I notice how warriors are organized
in kitchens both women & men
sip coffee & talk to mothers
sisters brothers & other first nations
the terrorism of my hosts is casual
but touches on an innerspring of silence
the blockade was truly amazing
because many people sobered up
put up with a shortage of baloney
fast foods and contraband groceries
every cupboard drawer became neat
& organized like Mercier Bridge

still it's not finished; demonstrations
will occur when the honeymoon is over
or should the pink lady get kids chaos
a different color scheme
her home if invaded once again
finicky housekeeping might even attract
not discourage the messmakers to drop by
I will merge better next time
check out sun deck surveillance
observe the foxtail detail

a cynic I tend to see grey linings
hid in pink socialist clouds
what doesn't compute is my duty
an inquiring mind wants to know
I get told the identity problem

is 100,000 Indians do not know
tribes of origin but make up lies
numbers make facts more credible
the pretended past does distract
I have tattooed the verification
of Indian status on my big toe
band number without the photo
I will show it if I'm ever asked
when I sneak behind the lines
next siege demo protest to help out
I have provable identity in case
clan membership expires annually
or my traditional but urban story
requires I reinvent my ancestors

I don't accept the easy Indian life
or counteract most rejections I get
how those who speak the truth
of their identity might say something
different unusual unbelievable
keep the story straight if it's a mystery
not everyone works for CSIS or CIA
I don't want everyone to be Indian
or to be too suspicious either
they should have interesting bric brac
with pristine impeccable backyards
keep on decorating interiors
I don't want to fight for exteriors
fight for home fight for sanctuary
defend status regained
a right to being Indian
is not a pretty picture
an identity made questionable
by invasion or evasion

Mother In the News

for Ann Weyaus

she is news: her right arm holds up
log big enough it broke the front window
she posed for the camera proud to tell
everyone in this part of town her rights
she won because she fought back fierce
a slum landlord, street punks, drunks

the fixed worry lines on her forehead
join two downward run grooves to lips
able to give a genuine grandma smootch

in the photo she has a short frizz perm
no stoic tranquil braids for her look
she don't play the instant elder role

her terrified girl story kept hidden
from the mother with a loaded gun
pointed at what now is a smiley face
she remembered that mother with tears
so we young ones would tell her forget
this misery mother needs to be told

get lost
     not wanted back mother
     unless you behave better
     more like a mother
she stayed a scared woman years after

tobacco is a gift to give to elders
but she gave out smokes we craved
how generous this woman got
since she told us her mother story

couple drags made my smoke cloud
under it I would also remember
the next to last time I saw my mother

she was supposed to visit me
that time she got out of jail
the Mother's Day card I bought
with satiny feel floral teapot
I pressed the sponge padded spot
up and down milking the belly
teapot for a mother daughter feel

my mother kept me waiting
for affection time after time
but that time got cut off short
a bartender drowned out her asking
more beer if bootlegger how much

closing time move along lady
closing down beer parlor woman
closing me up to close up looks

I just for the fun of it dust off
her memory   brush her bones
            ever tickley
make her fancy   laugh   again & again

I set up archeology expeditions
but digging up mom takes work
news of where did she go abandon me

I turn instead to faded old newspaper
clipping to brag about this fighter mom

this mom is not in a skeleton closet
not checked out in the obits mother

but my birth mother I find stuck in
heart shaped pincushion she made
I talk straight to buried needles
she left memories in me deep hurts
stab my heart velvet soft and worn

Four Directions After Her Life

*Dedicated to a parting of spirit
at Jocelyn House, Winnipeg*

Extinct her animal

She survives a skeletal but not sceptical poem. I see her lioness
kicked in the jaw, hunched down in a dry mud gully panting. Me,
the big lens. Close up. She clicks her dose of painkiller. Shoot over.
She waits for death and I give up Wild World of Animals obsession.
Told she was dying. I came to look.

Mother our secrets

She again will escape bad poetry nights. She'll squint at the blur on
what is left of a peeled beer bottle label. Mother words puncture her
hang over ear drums with tympani. Mothers we became. Imagination
makes do for shot up conversation with lies we told each other. Her
booze mother confronted mine. All-Star Mother Wrestling except
one died before treatment was invented. More mothers die for a
planet. Exit the poison environment mother. Her shrine is waste.
Wanted: a placebo poem mother. Plug in the dildo. Turn on the
appliance mom, shiny chrome sides to hold toast, brew a cup, or
spin dry, launder up generation shame blame.

Cant bear

Talk about bears on TV. Polar bears declared a protected species.
Why kill for a coat someone? Each animal I mention is almost
extinct. No talk about her dying. We both barely know bears. And,
bears know more about humping. Bears enjoy one another. Play
around. Even the quickie takes more time for them. Quickest lover
she ever had: answered a personal ad, came at the door, introduced

himself as he left. Missed out on the physical part. What if he just wanted a bear coat? Didn't want the bear. She must suffer suffocation under the heat of polar bear skin on humid day. Her heat. Her hot. Fur intact. Bears know how to die. Surrender hot gall bladders for someone else to heal.

Sweetgrass talks

Her Patsy Cline song made her walk after midnight. Sweetgrass makes walk same as talk. Whips around in the mind mother. Connects wild mouth organ back to the tongue. Should stick. Stay in place. Keep the tongue from prying open the coffin. Not out talked, let's hear one midnight singsong. Louder voices busy at last rites. She might rise from coffin to tell off shake'n'bake medicine man. She saw instant elder cult vulture inside his skin. Faked him out. Revealed his bogus ass face. Hey, pretty fake poem. At the funeral, I can't bear to read this poem I wrote for me not for her. Her poem rubbed off the beer bottle by sleight of hand. My poem robs a fur-bearing animal of dignity. Don't want to rub fur the wrong way. Keep between us mother talk. Daughter anger.

Geratric Canoe Princess

she poet alive
land the river
holds body parts
as if must let go
bundle of belongings

know this sister
when tide rises inside
pain stab in breast
spirit will release
even against embrace
fighting resistance
hate this place
let's get out of here
it's boring
nothing ever happens
especially where I'm involved

land slopes upward
rocky mountain cat paws
incisor gnaws
ripped skin
the purrs
belly full
she is slaughter
furlined mound
wingless feathers
scales shells bones
from shimmer water

her eyes witness
coast line constant
her tongue
lap lap lapping water edge

she is surmised
at sun rise
canoe chant
cedar switch
she traveler princess
paddle up water drops
shine splendor
the hurt will wash out
seaweed does the job

mister sister
okay so she lost my Indian
at Lost Lagoon

legend place
legend mind
legend woman
legend tells one

legend past
legend remote
legend self
legend tells two

legend island
legend water
legend travel
legend blabber mouths

legend sucks
legend pukes

legend composts
legend stays put

legend wakes
legend sleeps
legend vibrates
legend explodes

legend reads
legend newspapers
legend radio
legend brunch

legend stroll
legend beach
legend rock
legend cafe

legend ashes
legend death
legend ocean
legend lived on Homer Street

legend had breast cancer
legend had sex
legend had fun
legend will come

when was the last time
sex she means
this time a definite come

mind if I smoke in bed
smoke
as I watch foreplay
smoke up

as you huff and puff
smoke
myself to sleep
turn smoke meat
not rubbed raw
dance around my own fire
once I light up
send a smoke signal
from my own burning bush

she said one thing I hate
is an uncircumsised cock
downtown women's center
speaker went on to say
he bought drinks for her
in his hotel room made her look
scum rise think she said
he had it out for her

then someone said
if I had a paddle
I would have pounded him
Who's talking to you anyway
let the speaker interrupt
her own story

tell the one about Dead Woman's Island
or was that dead mother, dead sister, dead aunt
whatever sounds good to you
speaker chimed in
another late-breaking story
she didn't want to miss
becoming a headline
hey better than a deadline
she laughed
at would-be satin coffin

it's okay boys I know all
about how you took my skull
from cave
gave me away
to a museum
down south
my bones stretch
round the world

she was the ghost
seen before a person dies
the lookalike
the one who laughs too much
too loud too soon not enough

why spook us
why be vulgar
just to get attention
suppose she said
jump in my canoe
never mind the sea bus
you don't have time
trouble times we are all legend
if we know it or not
when we go by canoe
we remember to remember
we are remembered

RED NOISE

An Account of Tourist Terrorism

History is just used Pampers on the
grave of Sitting Bull at Yankton but
because of crushed beer cans, obvious
Lakota visitors to this historic site
know what is under the earth, the lake,
the Black cook who died the same day.
McLaughlin buried both in the fort
with quicklime to foul up those Mobridge
businessmen's rendezvous with the right
bones to connect to make one skeleton.
What is history and what did happen
is a deeper question than tourists
dumping dollars in an empty memorial.
The words not written on the plaque or
between the lines are ghostwritten graffiti.
Glow in the dark instructions if you dare
to landfill history, deposit postcards,
return artifacts, souvenirs and the clutter
of plastic tomahawks buried in our minds.
Indian raids are nothing in comparison.
Tourist terrorism is ceremony without fuss,
and who takes the bother stops desecration.

Woman Bath

Friday night at the old train station was our last communal bath

Then a little girl I was slept on a wooden bench waiting for a train to come or go but now even the health club will close down no more reconversions necessary or even possible because Main Street got too scuzzy and dirty not so for tourists

Main Street always a bad parade of all women in relations even Off Main on Austin Street hookers pass right on by me but they don't dare relate to me or my whitewomen buddies who came after the swedish massage not the corroded Saturday night bathtub   I get the picture of what it's like to be down Main Street not them

Before we exit the car we chat about non-white hooker found dead in a ditch this morning but we escape the truth of terrible city terrible men who frequent this skidrow street

I assume she was Indian she was disposable did I mean to say it like that because a year later I find she might have been from the next reserve   I might have been another stand-in auntie to her

My white friends are right that she was a coloured girl adopted into a white family just the other day a client of theirs she had her one mistake and mine is to believe their story in toto

We bathe together I like part where we washed off the news together class differences down the drain & naked women are equal even behind our towels I slung my towel on my hips tightly

One Eye Annie used to scavenge the hotel dining room got lips a bit greasy but was pitched back into the street by those with proper

protocol to welcome the Queen of England in the event she ever
became an old bag

An Indian woman leaned against a pillar jiggling tiny tits then slunk
back to white lovers who witness gay pride but   she doesn't
like me   funny how she changed her first name to mine though
I don't care for it enough to share this time

I didn't resist Other circles of white guilts to get out my dirt refused
to join up with women helping Clean up your own act I told them
but please keep in mind I mind my company dearies

I washed the shy side under my towel pretended to spy on a camp
Nazi women torture on command all the slim girls dancing for
them I watch helplessly   each seduction because I am afraid to
keep diets

Such dirty thoughts for an average non-white me but I scrub harder
white part of my pinto hide   got to scrub my geed too but I
cracked under pressure even that of my own hand

I need to take it easy I am too hard on myself they rush to tell me
when I think I am just about to figure it out

Half of me trekked off to the steam room spritzed by spray nozzle
one of me doesn't fit in a women crowd   often left in complete
rage because the white twin belonged better

Women read Tarot Runes for future plans ask questions about
abundance & working with Indian girls on the streets who need
extra rubbers sometime sexual workers give up luxuries prioritize
money life men even welfare

The cleansed one found the dirty one reclining on a cot looking
superior pure ridiculous unable to be appeased of fury   tempted
one follow the dirty old thing to a tunnel

Her pride swells investigates the exact places the girl danced for
white lovers social workers teachers nurses forget police women
when if she gets close

Curious I have been discussed as to how my racism prevents
treatments deserved by other Indian women tending to trust not
disappoint or please others who work for them

(Might become vapour molecules spread therefore I am sniffed)

Alice saw the Queen of Hearts playing croquet graciously Her
majestic Heart is well worn Her shoulders sag from extensive yoga
lessons to tolerate my potential quirk to play with Her mallet   I
will strike when it is actually my turn

Her inquisition face Her red tam One Eye Annie covered Her dead
eye She guides young hookers Her own daughter was spared Her
rape She tells Indian girls Her past but not Her daughter Her baby
won't listen like shy Indian girls she is immune to mom's dangers
mama speech patterns don't work because mamas will avoid pain or
what is on the agenda or what has to be told to each girl

Say Queen of Hearts or One Eye quit working with my sisters now
each one is mine & worth many zeros to fill a blank cheque that
won't bounce in my face & make cash now out of my sweat

I thought only men were the customers & I'll find turquoise colours
for each woman who is my sister I want sisters to like me

Dangly hoop earrings don't match or beaded quills are no better &
who wears my identify feminist fashion puts more rags on the back
of the dead girl

They didn't know her well enough or her race I spotted a non-
white person who never told anyone of her future as evident as it
was at the time but why bother to wake her up she rests her case &

will hear what happened in a roundabout peculiar way I must be
scrubbed empty

I found the dead girl in me   she wasn't killed by my words

Turtle Island Woman

Gary Snyder
wrote about Turtle Island
won a Pulitzer prize

whiteboy poetry
was all I didn't know much
what to write
for whom for why

he said thanks the one day
I gave him my poetry book
said "read this for a change"

Turtle Island woman gave heart
away to his ecological zone
he must give offerings
to a woman spirit
I know I read his poems
listen up for that woman

did he just say gimme to her
the glib coyote testimony way
is a give away

he tells me
white boys
claim to be artists first
like Indian are supposed to be
artists first
to write whiteboy stink

if we are artists first
then we don't need to be Original People
first is a first for first nations
we have to imagine Turtle Island Woman
with her borrowed green heart
not taken as outright steal

he'd refill his pen
greenish ink
pumps from her heart

she didn't sit full lotus
position beside him
mimicing his wife either

she bitched
I heard it too

The Art of Talking Indian Art Shows

Dear Ann Dear Abby letters advice
    on marital problems

Is it true Indians are better lovers?

Definite yes appeals to arcane common sense
    Indians have secrets
    passed down fathers to sons
    even a part-Kickapoo had no complaints
    from his wife

American Indian Movement activist testifies
    Indians are better lovers
    I have 12 kids to prove it

Indian lovers are impossible
one woman states a belief
    if someone was put on the earth
    to devote myself to
    maybe I could make Burt Reynolds happy

Indian love is cheap and easy
    Indians are my favorite hobby
    tourist season is slow
    plastic Indians cost $13 on the reservation

damn hard to appreciate the art of newpaper clippings
related to the bigger question
artistic statement
license disclaimer
how feminists have Indian men all wrong

slide show presentation is proof positive
parade of used Barbie dolls
bunch up around Cherokee Prince
even Honest Moose scores big
behind a Pin-Up Pony
where does Nuclear Appaloosa fit

what speaks for the artist shows me
ready to implode
be put in place
must remain quiet Big Red Brother knows all
sit way back in big enough pressure cooker
especially donated by Presto for occasion
any moment an Indian woman makes it a hobby
tells all writes it down beyond the art of talking
is witness to recovered memory of lies beneath her

Condom Nation

Devine him say on night news hell on wheels
him mus be scare aids to bite pon our heels
First Nations no axe condom nations lak dis
we know whitemon spread disease him tongue curse
pon us put he rubber put he raincoat him first
jus condemn nation coz no more fun sex outside
relation mek extra Devine him stop verbal attack
pon us condom shoppers dat do el snag partytime
select extra strong latex dat don burst no leak
donate spare rubber to best lover den don freak
if we carry bout extra it mek travel extra light
case we stuck with safe permanent partner in life
buy dem by case condom never fraid store be close
why don't Devine hand out free tubes quit scare us
don dis first nation first wid more condom nation

Got Something In the Eye

Morbid finding a body in a ditch edge of town. Mirrored disco ball lodged in eye socket. Glamour eyeball throws dots of light from ceiling to floor. Swirl around in shadows. Dance round with shut eyes.

Typical tumbleweed guy. That dazzle eye looks impressive on a police cruiser. Hypnotize. Arrest. Interrogate. Chill out. Warriors on the street looking for political party. War party. Join any party since the last one wasn't greatest ever party. Keep in mind life doesn't have to be a party.

Last I saw him he was practicing dealer phone stance. His claim to fame was writer working on the next novel. Drunk and disgusting came later with offer of special discount price Only five frog skins. Boozer breath too much.

Speculative fiction not the I files. If he survives celebrity status, then long live Daddy Cyclops.

Learn to become victim and statistic after one Saturday night performance. Advantage author. Disadvantage audience. Hold on. He never looked up to his own kind. Publisher cranked out Indian books. Portrait on cover made so easy to hitch a ride.

The ball had to land on his face. Asked him was he alright. He assumed I wanted fisticuffs. Right left right out of it. Interfere with tough ex-con act. Eye eye eye amigo. Better approach from our blind spot.

The Mandan Hidatsa held two creators responsible for the mess of the world. The perfectionist located the wolf carcass full of maggots. Then he confronted the other creator about the botch job. Maybe this way someone much better at defects gets reminded of truest creation.

Exercises in Lip Pointing

Okay today
let's have the lips speak for themselves
shall we let them say what they must
say if asked
if ever asked
as if anyone ever asks
just the lips to speak
                    because the totality
                    of a person counts more

dominates
        what the lips want
                koochy koo lips
                lips pursed
        lips pointed full forward tilt
        top lip extended

signals

        watch ahead to the side
        either side
        take a peek

but don't say anything out loud
to Mr Mrs Ms Authority Person In Charge

        don't say   aw fuck off either
        you bug me   aw come off it
        enough enough
        that bullshit

ever hear the one
about what the one lip said to the other

                        ridiculous if
                        ever heard
                        one lip talk

point out impossible wish
if one had one wish

                    rapid lip movements as if talking
                    lips walking
                    to the convenience store

                    back alley lips
                    holding a cigarette
                    unable to scream
                    get that damn paper toxic
                    tobacco product out of me

exception none

        a language probes   prods
        asks all the right questions right
        meets its match in lips
        that won't respond in kind
                    sorry lips droop and sag
command
        lips move
                    quick march
                    single up
        form a circle around the wagons

        hey lips over there doing nothing
        lips don't pout
        grab those arrows
        start firing

lips on the other side of face
light a few guided missiles

to Hell with Tomahawks
let's Scud doo

what a range
lips lips lips
hold formation

lips keep still
mike's on
quiet on set

somebody might hear
somebody already knows
what lips to listen for
what lips to look out for

snarl Elvis lip
lip shake lips

lips don't betray
stop that quiver
stop that whimper

blubbering
how many times have you
lips been told to say

now just how many of you
at attention
just a couple last count
surrounded in ambush lips
lots of lips surrendered

lips lips hold back tighten
tighten up your ranks
files empty
yet not one word gets through

remember the cowboy Indian movie
                         especially starring in it

don't get lines
just come out trilling
give us lots of tongue
pow wow lips
contest time
ceremonial lips action

like how do you do that poise
make more noise make me notice you
                            biting too much
                            ouch sado-macho

stop stoic lips
stop bleeding heart
winding down whine lips
if there's one thing else

try to keep shut

JJ Bang Bang

I told you
stop in your tracks
give me your name address &
why you are walking on the street

THIS JUST IN
Today a Native woman was arrested
for standing on her porch. She was
taken into custody and placed in a
room with a couple having sex. She
is suing the police for false arrest. It is
unknown whether she is of Sioux
descent. She could be just another
Native woman.

why are you not impressed
why are you not listening
I said give me your identity
or else JJ Bang Bang

POLICE DOUBLE DITCHED
A cruiser was found in the ditch this
morning. The occupants were not
present to give a complete report to
fellow officers. Their inability to
walk a straight line made it difficult
for the police dogs to follow in
pursuit.

I told you go back up north
quit hanging around here
get off the streets

get a job go to school
you need a counselling referral
I want to see you in detention

FILM AT ELEVEN
A policeman, it is believed, chased a
stolen car suspect, an unlicensed
inexperienced 13-year-old driver. A
collision ensued when he hit a van.
He remains in hospital with sustained
ego injuries counting the bullet holes
in his chest received from a prior
attempt to arrest a copkiller.

I told you stop accusing me
my job is to look after you
but I'm not responsible to you
just for you your damn nation
give me good reason, one, why
I feel guilty what happens
to you when you go out wandering
alone at night

got a joke for you JJ Bang Bang
want to see me wink at you
cross my path, boy, hey put down
that cross boy

trouble with you natives
you're not good enough
too "mixed up" blood too damn
white like me not enough me
in your blood like me in your face

you never spoke up
when I had my hand down your pants

put your mouth where it belonged
boy I said suck me, boy
you suck up that government money
make those lips do your job
I'll do your talking
talk politic to my dick
JJ Bang Bang

hey, don't squirm on me, boy
just remember my foot on your neck
gotta rest my feet, my white load
better yet, turn around bend over
when I say reach for mother earth
dig in, surprise is behind you

JJ Bang Bang
when you do me chief
you move smooth you dancing
drum beat you tight as a drum
boy winding on my hard on
harder get me off you
make me off you get off you
off you sweet little boy
boy o boy

that kind they had in schools
those dirty priests
give me a big whoop JJ Bang Bang
what's your pleasure boy
going down going down
got a bullet
think I dropped my bullet down there
pick it up your name's on it

JJ Bang Bang
I'm going crazy without you
keep going down the street
can't take it anymore chief
stress pressure being me
being better than I believe
I'm ever going to be
but you look through
my uniform see rank file
authority I put my gun
in your ribcage
I want this publicity for you
my trigger happy finger
not my fuck you finger

so arrest me JJ Bang Bang
show me your badge, son
come take my gun
it makes my gitch itch to kill

JJ Bang Bang
when you die do it slow
bleed into the pavement
bleed into my mind
damn that's a lotta alcohol
you bleeding numb son of a bitch
Indian you let a cop kill you
not one of your own boys

AMERICA'S MOST WANTED
One cool morning about 5 a.m.
several men surrounded an Indian on
the Ten Most Wanted list. He was
killed before police were on the
scene to make proper identification
of the suspect.

A reward is offered for any information leading up to this crime. Is his mother to blame? Was he a multiple victim?

Was he an Indian for sure or just a Métis? Criminal status not easy determined as if he has status or not.

after you're dead JJ Bang Bang
I'll make your wife confess
write a letter say you are
a better wife beater than me
my friend at detox saw you
trying to pick up a woman
brought in for being a loudmouth

MUKYTOON TIMES
After a lengthy inquiry police need
time to fabricate events records heal
go to sweat lodges pow wows
next police class is at least half Native
but native what?
half Native part pig siouiii
Aboriginal cop out

not long ago, 50 young people
surrounded a Native youth who was
believed to be beaten up by them
until the police came after it was
over to get details.

Prisoner of My Poem

In jail I am the concrete. I scratch my name into the thin rubber mattress pad beneath me. I might even stay the night but that glass sliding door doesn't keep out the groans or a call for the matron.

I start bawling humiliated by the hygienic measure of an Indian matron who searched me because she had been especially hired to touch me. I won't be calling on her for a blanket. She didn't feel my crotch — her job. I'm sure a whitelady would've jumped at the opportunity.

I may leave anytime because I turned myself in. I may decide to astral project myself home. I will see the cats run up to me. They are curious rub on my legs but will lean through my form. I will check to see if the door is locked even as I float through the frame.

I try switching channels to see how my favorite poet sprawls on her bed with 13 cat fur mounds. My precious spot is taken. They ignore my circling to make myself comfortable.

I'm a special case. I notice mostly Indians in jail even though it was claimed that college grads and the mayor become incarcerated on occasion.

Time before the last time I was in jail with Mr. Common Assault. My husband rounded up after I asked if my crime was worse than his. We both ended in lock up for beating me up. He got out first. The only reason I left with him was I needed a smoke not him.

One voice busts into my cell asking what is my name what am I in for will I get out soon but I lie the fine is too embarrassing. Rent money made the cops say I had enough to give them. I am a fine enough Indian with money. She told me she was the uttering kind. Uttering is a crime.

I'm from a skid row amusement park. I've seen the cinch pinch an authentic cop show down to drunk Indian arrest. Back then my uncle flat on his back on the sidewalk said his name was King George VI. Making us laugh. They poked him with billy clubs but they didn't do the RCMP jig on him.

I have since worried about the crime rate. Would I be robbed or raped? I have to turn over on my back to get comfortable. It's hard to think about crime when locked up.

If my friend asks me next time I get picked up if I wrote a poem about being in jail I will read her this one and ask her if she might loan me money for the fine or come down to get me out of this poem.

Who Am I to Judge

Conversation at the next table
in a Vietnamese restaurant
a family court judge happens
to be a psychiatric nurse
and a social worker too
but he's not overqualified
he didn't talk to a Native woman
lately who lost kids

I hear it's rude to enter
private conversations
rude to keep listening
rude
unless the topic attracts
it's not that rude
I throw in my two bits
to them I'm invisible
know we haven't been talking
to and/or about a Native woman
lately who lost her kids

I'd make a poor defence
not one to shield her
from the judicial x-ray stare
or conceal the whole truth
white noise is used for torture
the sloshing in my stomach
gives away my presence
the gurgle is in resistance
to white noise in the background

I'm guilty I didn't cook at home
I confess to sweet and sour soup
slurped over a six month period
picked this night to dine out
to overhear curious conversations
offensive to my favorite cuisine

It's a crime a judge won't condemn
or hear testimony about too often
but still he'd make me pay
take those mental notes
my eyelid has excess thickness
the brown eye itself slants
Mongolian eyefold identification
he'd seen this problem from the bench
knows the sentence to fit the eye contour
no fine option or community service
I'm sure it's not about unpaid fines
the soup is cheap and excellent
naturally, I will overrule him
his table of subordinates are served
first by a waitress who has those eyes

who am I to judge this guy
except I hear the mothers
outside the courtrooms
heard complaints from a few
fit to judge mothers
frequent court appearances
has changed my testimony
I am a mother not a judge
mothers are left out of conversations
words about eyes that look down
or up or similar to Gengis Khan,
Bruce Lee and Charlie Chan

I want to enter those conversations
debate on how he or his wife
sister sweetheart co-worker buddy adopted
"papooses" from up north who return
for adult sentencing
some adoptions are slavery
in my jurisdiction I'd arrest anyone
obstructing a mother

I'm aware of how rude it is to mention
a weak reputation on the part of the judge
maybe he is an unfit judge
his record, his resumé, his reference
wouldn't slip by me without notice

I exploit the Native woman issue
especially those lately who lost kids
exploit this cause to raise up
rude thoughts I should keep
silent vigil

let all the mothers jump up jump in
jump on his honor, investigate his case

I wish the Native woman lately
who lost kids would drop in here
say something to ruin his reputation
shoot straight arrows into his back

it's rude enough to ruin my dinner
the white noise at the next table
I want to shush them quiet, complain
typical racist ambience ruins a dinner out

it must've happened to Native women lately
more often to those who lose

custody of kids
white noise is how they talk
about just us
never just him, just her or just me

How to Stop Writing About Indians

A friend taught me the significant details
how to roll my own whiteguy
     simple enough
yet I let the video camera
         distract me
my trust won; he kissed up to me more

eventually I found out, withdrew myself
my contribution to our local writing union

     me

     my story

told him one dark night I might meander
inside his head to write my award winner
quote his Indian buddy who said it best
"first the poison." Given enough poison
Indians will die out but who will give us
the secret remedy or cure for bad writing?

How to Write About White People

From a distance & keep them outside
even if it seems cruel to do that.
They will sit on the prairie horizon
left to silouette as grain elevator
once you rode up on a spotted stallion.

The inner Trojan fears kept them
talking too much about the country they took.
Look how rats took over the greedy stores.
Grain sprouts grew outside walls of wooden wars.

Pony charger nibbles on blades brushed by hooves.
Bannocks were white seeds kept in towers.
We never climbed up to the top but rats did.

The white chief told me he ran from the city.
He was made lumpy and grumpy.
Innoculations were frequent.
They tried every day to kill him.
Psychology was what they called the war.

Laboratory used to be his first name.
He changed his address after the millenium.

Saskatchewan Indians Were Dancing

60s pulled us from starvation into government jobs
antiquated Indians in Saskatchewans danced for rain
Manitoba Indian doings were hidden for a jealous me
all I had was a 50s rock'n'roll step to copy from
not shy you danced for strangers from deep defiance
full regalia hid other dangerous rope dancing kicks
Crees got out of line on the scaffold teaching Cree
readiness to enter the earth at the exact spot left
following a song trail maybe even a we want a chant
chant after teasing hey boy you first boy first one
dancing in the air show them how to teach us lesson
a public display of rationed revenge serves nothing
show example to culture clashed passive politicians
Crees hit them notes higher boys cover up ear drums
let other drums beat out natural powwow exhibitions
boys in the pen idle for a time listen up flag song
Cree hit parade will release some traditional lives
dancing not allowed behind bars then songs bring us
back to good times Saskatchewan Indians danced free

COYOTRIX RECOLLECTS

The Can Is Busy

Wait here, the can is busy she tells me
too many drunks around these parties.
Nevermind. I'm going outside by myself.
I don't need protection to go to the can.

Many stars out as I stagger in cold air.
Kept occupied finding my zipper.

He must have got used to all the people.
No excuse me, he stuck his big nose in.
He must be known for doing this trick.
We were known to that horse by our anatomy.

Barking dogs escorted me back to the house.

Lady Buddha Intent

Verna Lyons memorial

need no umbrella   rain soaked city morning
Lady Buddha presides   need no umbrella
forecast for Vancouver is damp

S&M bar sweetgrass burns in a shell
feather carries smoke to swirl every woman face
anxious person asks what next what next
next to me a woman who knows each circle
bleeds comfort when a fat moon slivers down

Japanese women with split white toe socks drum
white deer feet in a circle of feet round dance move

hooker feet in heels
gay feet with boots
Anishinabekwe feet
moccasin mileage walk talk

moon-curved shell earring fell off my earlobe
giveaway
offering at vigil will stroll the sky
keep company with Lady Buddha
dangle on a long stretched ear
decorate circle altar
women benefit

grief shared

tears close the bar business
women held hands make ceremony
spirits travel ad infinitum
ever and ever buddy system

where our path breaks off
Lady Buddha intent will take over
splash grounds

dry eyes indulge a soul stare
never the time we overdose empathy
pity loss no rubber ducky

no umbrella covers up the entire body

rain gathers in gutters
puddles of water cleanse
we walk the same streets she did
Lady Buddha preside please
slight wetness on skin
light rain trickles our way

Even Raven Has Hang Ups

don't I know you from somewhere?

wing flutter feather fuss
how dare I question black authority ripple sheen guy

your somersault squirrel fashion
roughing up leaves and hanging
upside down caught my gaze

no answer except to cock head
twist peek sideways

do you always wear black?

formal dress for dinner invite
he pretends to stalk a worm
I order dinner for one person
watch him appear indignant
through a restaurant window

the outfit matches your beak

better to spear into dark earth under lawn greenness
but hold the distraction I overlook how he stabs again
take up my fork poke push
cubed welldone steak morsels
he shifts foot position angst
keeps poking the ground furious fashion
I lift my fork up down up down

beak agape is too cute

heavy hopping on dark earth
brings no results much too eager
master flirt quits to fly up
reassure the tree perched mate
she looks over his suave touch
safe he gets no warning peck
waiter brings peach melba
rapid spoon thrusts
dissect treat raven deserts me

chill out, raven, no
I'm won't go talking you up

he airs his damp wing pit
flaps up feathers in display
I expect the show starts soon
so he attempts a vertical lift
to finish with glide descent

raven, you deserve hang ups

when we meet in public I act casual
as if meeting you for the first time
know how you raven
sneak up romance
between you an appetizer
then me as dessert

Dropped Shorts

whose shorts these
what a day what night
shorts dropped tease
why had been had
on 1st and Commercial
crosswalk between banks

translation if ever
what about this
gitch on the pavement
what voice over narration
nobody around here says
or throws underwear away
could be recycled

Write Off

he took off so early without words
birds banged into windows
of the restaurant
ate my breakfast
half belief I saw them

he wrote long letters
travelled by bus to visit

he was serious minded
except his chair tipped over
at a strip show in Denver

last time I saw him
he drank only his beer
I cooked dinner
his teeth were gone
he said so I felt better

admired his carved feast spoon
he couldn't chew meat
but he told old scary stories
made me respect

watch out
watch out
bear walk

whiteman trap
his brandy snifter
full again

he'd continue
his name meant
clouds sneaking up
storm coming
say your Indian name

you hung around
to tease us
kept us humble
about the writing game
the stories we lived

I Shoulda Said Something Political

you spoke to me Emilia   I chiquita
tiny bit lick paste on label   you compañera
green tinge pretty banana   wait for ripe
yellow chiquita skin moment   takes more
than Spanish descent I mean   to be decent
descend   even the imported banana gets mushy

hey, hey, celtic conquistadora   my ancestry
a search for potatoes   why have a famine
in the first place I say   I ask how about you
where you come from   we have it in common
so far away do you happen on a feast often
grab a clean plate   sit down next to
talk to someone like me   talk turkey

I'm so serious   cute tomato   how you gave
them yourself   had to had to   so did I
me too, I shared so I did   I share more
did you forget the gold   did you did you
give it away   the gold chain
my friend gave me to wear   gets in the way
when I eat   my fingers catch it   put it
in my mouth   so you passed the ketchup
to them   too bad it happens   squashed tomatoes

we are just delicious   they put us on
french fries I gave up   potatoes to make poutine
now that's strange   does it have much blood
any barter   taste enough gravy

you sprawl next to me   long legs   log jam
look you harvested timber   you fall

your arms reach across miles   how do you
do that trick   for agricultural sake
you fondle the cornsilk   kiss up pumpkin vine

your anatomy & mine   separate from what belongs
to the Mohawk tobacco trader   asks for a light
gets up to smoke outside the lodge   we see him
give offering of tobacco   pray   we watch him
without him to watch us play   entangle
human sculpture   should he take notice be bold
scold after doing righteous act   gotta brace
for trouble   entwine legs arms minds
if he comes back without smokes   let's behave
give thanks for lights   surprise spirit sparks

how queer for you, for me to lay back   wonder
the rest of the summer   I lazy ass down
druggy park kept vigil unlike   outhouse poet
behind the treatment center   kept folks
occupied, safe   he loved laughs and war alike
it occupied my mind   no fierce risky business
stopped my preoccupations   gross everyone out
arouse oppositions   shoulda been the poet
at Oka, sneak up in monk habit   fire words
take the straight forward approach   fire at
choppers   write poetry on walls waste less
paper, words   maybe Emilia, I apologize

should go to Peru   accompany each other
be safe escorts   for us mixed up together
just us tourists   in blond California wigs
dark Barbie twins   shining our hair
right shampoo   the Shining Path   economy
we set up a stall to sell   big words
to fatten the skull   trepinate paths
poem trouble again   I instead

made myself comfy   lying on railway track
to blockade national trains   gave support
warriors need more uplift   hard curve balls
pitched   at their athletic supporters
makes me wince groan ow   my fast lips came
in handy where it should be   the groin
talking   such Indian woman heterophobia

that summer   I just missed it   had to be
there to catch a great conference   needed
the proper lesbian lovemaking   establish
Indian men higher awareness   now
that's revolution   maybe it will happen

in Peru the altitude does it   guaranteed
an identity   that doesn't split sexes up
first time dropped   nothing breaks out
sags, or leaks   the victim in you refuses
everything that happened before   doesn't

want explanations   make it right for others
be a non-statistic   be understood
in the marketplace   let's for once
inside you let that jaguar purr   asleep
she shifts leg but inside growl   deep
I hear it compañera   growl dark like me

Squaw Pussy

Jaguar women in black Jaguar car

dispel typical "squaw" image
Hollywood Indian princesses
with braids & dowdy looks
instead upwardly mobile perms
replace primitive outlooks
expected in our stealthy climb
upward the snakey ladder
each rung writhing tales
forked feminist fables
hiss story, more hiss than story

Cool strong positive Anishinabekwe

knows her place is workplace
maybe she brings friends
to ride her new Jaguar to the bank
cash another cheque
she wants a lift from the past
best available frontier screw
squaw pussy zigzagged miles
on and off our backs
without tender ties or lies
the west was won
no, don't douche your doubts
or skirt your horizons
Squaw Pussy was powerful
saved a woman from drudgery;
pounded pemmican, tanned leather
beaded footwear sales

Our Cinderella born Native

has sizzling moccasins to fit
her stroll on a cement prairie
glass slippers are too fragile
to keep on her historic route

Our First Nations business woman

pulls off her negative image
tugging a travois behind tribe
she won't follow a white lady's
long haul behind man or plow

Study: Winnie the Pig With Seagulls

The seagulls circle around the block
double back follow hide in apartment hallways
lurk in a church basement
old devious gull   elastic bands hold up cut off
trousers at the knee to exhibit how flaccid
don't look down but notice how his wooly coat
has expensive lining   he hums he haws

The guy with homburg   fidgets with it on his lap
routine he wanks on a bus   he's not one who caught
a woman's silk scarf in his zipper   upon innocent
check on his fly   embarrassing enough exposure
in the free press would cure these guys
from the small towns or suburbs   flash of face
before they set out to work each morning
because at night   flocks cruise streets toss bible
in glove compartment

Open Wider

Open wider says the dentist and I remember when I did.
It's a push, pull, and drag sale on a TV commercial.
I spot a rapist selling used cars. He did push apart,
pull my legs underneath him. He dragged me to the bushes.
He was after a cherry that night but twenty years later,
he deals used goods. I hear his open wider voice again.

The rubber dam in my mouth and drug makes me follow the
lyrics to *Hit the Road, Jack* on the radio. Not a favorite
tune of mine because I didn't call out for help,
or make a scene more difficult. I remember how to sing
it under the breath when he's done with me. I feel not
much pain in my mouth from holding back my scream. That
song was a hit. The silenced scream hides in the throat.

This dentist amuses me with his talk about my tooth as
any old bad guy. He says "we'll fix this guy — we'll get
this character."

Red Bro Share This One With Me

Creator made you equal to me
behind bars you act the big man
you equal whatsoever fear how free
outside I must walk at your side

you follow what you memorize
in your meetings day in day out
you hear the first rib story
Adam forced to be generous
Eve was made outta secondhand rib

now we do share to give both of us
a little extra bit of life
your life right now is caged
inside an animal teased to rage

judges and lawyers get extravagant
poke our bellies to examine our loss
derive thrill from fat heart in custody
taken home from foster home nothing
but the usual fatherless revenge plus

it all adds up to windigo feast
a famine of children
the system ate them
spit out a bone

Red Bro
you had to be here
not there

Me Tonto Along

My old man was a good screw they say
all the ladies who chanced his waylay
he took my money time any hour he pleased
cost me to see how his manhood freezed
kicked him out he kicked down the door
punched my face through the apartment floor
no way to stop him but once he caught zzz's
had my chance to plot his murder with ease
I pretend I let him move on to a next wife
Me Tonto along what I got left — my life

Call Me Grey Wolf

He asks me to help him remember the little kid
he was. I found a suitjacket his size in the Goodwill.
Because he played at marriage when he was only five.
He told the bus driver he knew about marijuana.
When the train conductor yelled next stop Regina,
he woke me saying "Hey Mom, that guy said vagina."

He wanted the name Grey Wolf. I told him the story
how he got his bear clan name Day Seeker.
A bear seeks out the light after a winter sleep.
But he liked the name Grey Wolf better.
He read it in a book at the daycare.

He asks tough questions. I still give weak answers.
We admire two stuffed wolves displayed in the lobby.
The showcase sign says coyotes take habitat advantage
over grey wolves. I heard coyotes will mate
freely with dogs to have wild puppies that bark.
I call him part coyote, part puppy and wolf too.

Dad's Zipper

My father's fingernails got more brittle
and curved under. I trim them back
when he asked. Twist his thumb back
and make sure to use the pointy scissors.

He was proud of the black hightop runners
he wore without laces. Cost him six bits.
Gave him slippers but he wears them to please
me and his grandson when we visit.

He tied a shoelace to the zipper tab
in case he had trouble opening his fly.

It Was Like

666 Beast of Welfare
end of millenium
to get a cheque
takes an apocalypse
too much time

mini-money slide
off the finer
dinosaur egg embryo
flop on pavement

jelly around
with partial shell

now Alien critter
might run out of carbos
or what fuel or food
or fucks it takes
to fuck itself in dignity

today the package of twenties
landlord has to pick up

rent time was two weeks ago
old lady downstairs
go between me last time warning
not nice I stay hid distance

this cheque day was the last day
on earth if angels wanted to sing

soul music feathers aflight
wings aflap do wop

this resurrection will do for now

shopping for a cheque
no I don't want this one
it's too big too small
too outta style
too too too much

waiting for survival
has to be worth it
very merry happy joy

solo big cheerio rolls
bumps the curb
wobbles
winds down

a poem ago
became teacher screech
fleeced out wooly minds
excepted intercepted
without much class
if did or ever say so

still wait for cheque
middle of month
food bank week
weak from wait
hate it yet crate it refuse
no waiter or server
takes masses of volunteers
for chase down baloney sandwich

landlords are beasts
665 or 667 kind
commercial drive
is about money
capitalism drive by

not what's under the cap
ism front and back

Westcoast Meeting at the Bus Depot

Bus depots used to be Indian hangouts
gay pick-up places
agree to meet a westcoast poet
act the whiteman's guide
tag behind a poet going to a bookstore
see what happens when poets visit
where does the poetry come from
especially when poets travel by bus
to help the poems along

look his poetry over
a choice of wearing police boots
possibly match with stomped Natives
but go with faded blue jean
ribboned boniness

more than travelling memorabilia
he brings Pauline Johnson message
long ago her ashes dissolved in sea
I divined her essence once
she visits me again
I ate crumpets near her spot
drank tea by the Siwash Rock
sat on the shore
tranced
spirit dance
no but reflected light in water
pulled me toward her movement
needed more dope to face
my alien sense
at the meeting place

under the Lion's Gate Bridge
somehow I wanted to be lower
skid further into the call of the paddle sing
become one humble poem
chuck myself out to sea &

I Want to Dance Wild Indian Black Face

I want to dance with the five tribes of wild Indians. Them Wild Magnolias, Golden Eagles, Golden Stars, Black Eagles and Young Sons of Geronimo dance wild Indian black face. I want to hear the crowd say "Ooh, them Indians are pretty today."

I want to see a tribal official ready to lead his gang into battle like Council Chief, Second Chief, Trail Chief and Wild Man.

I want to shout back wild calls and big boasts of Big Chiefs in uptown New Orleans. I want to shout in my own city rez way.

I want to play in an inner circle of raggedy rhythm with beat-up drums, cowbells, tambourines, whistles, wine bottles and sticks.

I want to carry on in a parade to sing Two Way Pak E Way. In Cajun, "Tuez bas qu'ou est" means "Kill anyone who gets in the way." I could be a mean Indian some days.

I want to honor the spirits of Black Indians and Choctows, Cherokees, Natchez and Seminoles who resisted the slave masters.

I want to wear a turkey feather in my hair and join the tribe of the Creole Wild West. I don't want to be authentic all the time.

I want to be a Tribal Hawk. Sing some jazz gospel ratty chanting. Shout my spirit. Claim black and blues brothers same as sisters.

I want to mask Indian, adopt the Indian spirit figure once a year dance in public with my big black face and talk back to chiefs.

I want to dance wild Indian blackface. I want to be that big bad black Indian in a carnival parade. I want an Indian day off.

Red Stone Lake

red stones find
Red Lake shore
speckled pink granite
okay wash stones
water's edge
put new finds in small pouch
toss out ones that split
half   toward duck
afloat   current
sinks deep underneath
other half polished by sand dune
rough edges go   sing split stone
twice as hard
takes toes to mix
tiny shells
with sand
black seaweed

tide brings all broken stones
to land up on the gravel road
pot holes journey rough
flies bite ankles
run up ridge of sand
pushed high
waves
north blowing breeze

stones incubate promise
sanctuary
stay for
coming home ceremony

first nations
welcome
      Red Lake pebbled beach

    bring canoes full of fish
    sand sifting wind
    Anishinabeg

    lake after lake scatter

    stones on shore

    carry stones to the city
    stop first run down tipi
      drop them one by one
      cooking stones
          bubbles burst
      kettle boils
    pink granite turn
      red stone
         take us
       back to red stone lake